Literacy World

Reading and Language Skills Book 1

When you see this symbol it means you will need a copy of the book.

Contents

Novel
Very Best Friend
Synonyms	Word	4
Adverbs	Word	5
Plurals	Word	6
Punctuating Direct Speech	Sentence	7
Verb Tenses	Sentence	8
Expanding Sentences	Sentence	9
Mapping out Events	Text	10
Quotes and Characters	Text	11
Story Openings	Text	12

Novel
Mrs Maginty and the Cornish Cat
Using a Dictionary and a Thesaurus	Word	13
Root Word Game	Word	14
Adverbs in Dialogue	Word	15
The Language of Rosie's Knight	Sentence	16
First or Third Person?	Sentence	17
Double Negatives	Sentence	18
Grandad: A Character Portrait	Text	19
Reviewing a Book	Text	20
Story Structure	Text	21

Short Stories
Dark Secrets
Idioms	Word	22
Empathizing With Zak	Text	23
Word Order	Sentence	24
Simile and Metaphor	Text	25
Chapter Challenge	Text	26
Using Commas	Sentence	27
Describing Events in a Story	Text	28
Apostrophes	Sentence	29
Writing in the Style of the Author	Text	30

Short Stories
The Chilli Challenge and Other Stories
Adding Suffixes	Word	31
Clauses	Sentence	32
Investigating Texts	Text	33
Connectives Linking Clauses	Sentence	34
African Life	Text	35
Changing the Ingredients	Text	36
Glossary of Australian Words	Word	37
Checking Agreement	Sentence	38
Different Points of View	Text	39

Plays
Odysseus and the Cyclops and Other Plays
Homophones	Word	40
Onomatopoeia	Word	41
Heroes in Greek Mythology	Text	42
Direct to Indirect Speech	Sentence	43
Performing a Play	Text	44
Setting the Scene	Text	45
Prepositions	Sentence	46
Writing for the Town Crier	Sentence	47
Writing From a Poem	Text	48

Novel: **Very Best Friend**

Synonyms

> **Synonyms** are words which have the same or nearly the same meanings. *e.g. kind — thoughtful, caring, helpful, good*

A Beardie's owner has been **cruel** to him. (page 40)

Copy this brainstorm. In the bubbles, write as many synonyms as you can for the word **cruel**.

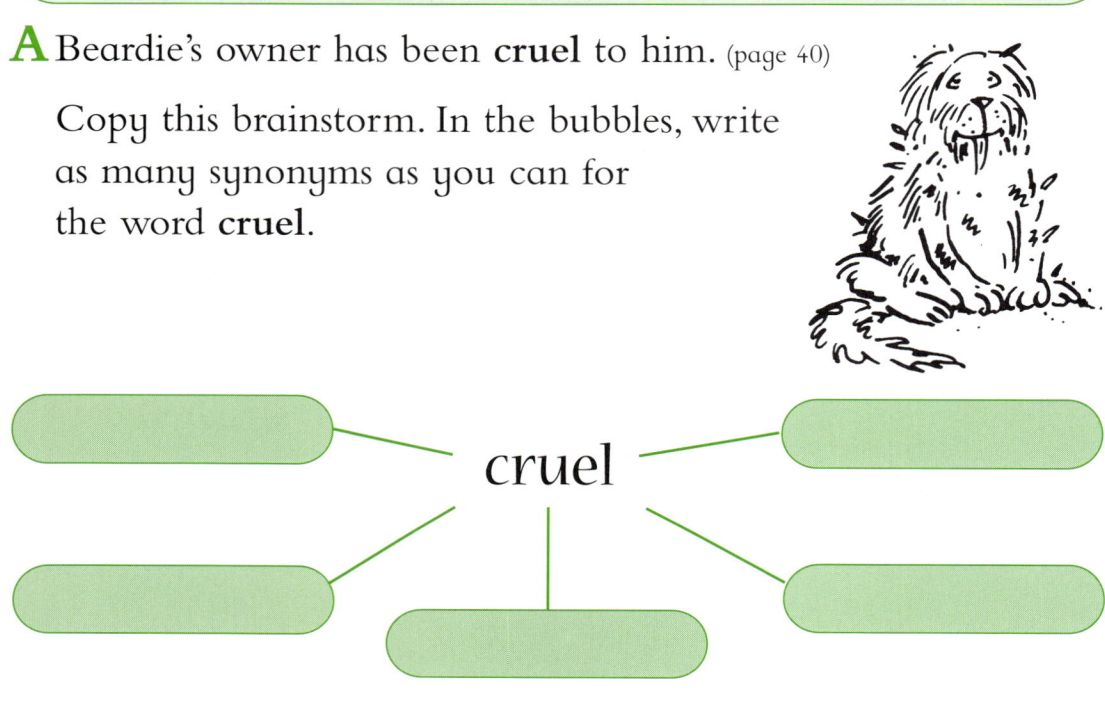

> Synonyms have shades of meaning, that is, slight differences from the least to the most powerful. *e.g. big, huge, enormous*

B Write these synonyms in order from the least to the most powerful.

1 good, all right, perfect
2 brutal, unkind, thoughtless
3 sad, devastated, upset
4 small, tiny, minute

C Choose one of the lists of words in section B. Write one sentence for each word.

4

Novel: *Very Best Friend*

Adverbs

> **Adverbs** can be used to describe how a character is speaking. *e.g.* 'Hello cats,' Ted said **shyly**. (page 6)

A Find the adverb in each of these sentences and write it down.

1 'Who sent you?' the dog asked huskily. (page 15)

2 'No one. I came myself,' said Ted gently. (page 15)

3 'He has been bad to you,' said Ted slowly. (page 17)

4 'I just know,' Ted answered mysteriously. (page 20)

Read aloud the sentences above in the way the adverb tells you. *e.g. Read number 1 in a husky voice!*

B Read these sentences. Write an adverb to describe how each character is speaking.

1 'Do you mean me?' asked Ted _____ 'But I'm not a giant.' (page 4)

2 'I don't know what I can do,' said Ted _____ . (page 24)

3 'Now I'll probably never see Beardie again,' said Ted _____ . (page 54)

4 'Oh there you are, Ted,' said Mum _____ . (page 59)

Novel: **Very Best Friend**

Plurals

> To make words plural:
> - add **s** to most words e.g. cat — cat**s**
> - add **es** if words end in **ch**, **sh**, **x** or **s** e.g. lunch — lunch**es**, dish — dish**es**, fox — fox**es**, moss — moss**es**

A Copy these words and write the plural of each.

1 bird – birds   4 patch   7 lioness

2 dog   5 wish   8 bush

3 branch   6 box   9 rhinoceros

> To make a word ending in **y** plural:
> - add **s** if there is a vowel (a, e, i, o, u) before the **y** e.g. boy — boy**s**, tray — tray**s**
> - change the **y** to **ies** if there is a consonant before the **y** e.g. family — famil**ies**, baby — bab**ies**

B Copy these words and write the plural of each.

1 toy   4 bay   7 holiday

2 cry   5 sky   8 berry

3 way   6 fly   9 buy

C Make lists of words ending in **ch**, **x** or **y**, and write the plural of each.

e.g. church – church**es**   mix – mix**es**   play – play**s**

Novel: *Very Best Friend*

Punctuating Direct Speech

When **punctuating direct speech**:
- speech marks go around the words characters say
- use a comma before the first set of speech marks
- put punctuation before the last set of speech marks
  e.g. Ted said, 'Hello cats.'
  'Oh, so you decided to speak to us!' said one cat.

A Copy these sentences, adding speech marks and punctuation.

1 Leave some for me said a tiny voice.

2 Does he feed you asked Ted.

3 You'll have to kidnap the dog Mouse told him.

Compare your answers with the story. The quotes can be found on: Quote **1** (page 3), **2** (page 16), **3** (page 25).

B Write this conversation between Ted and Beardie the dog as direct speech. The first part has been completed for you.

'Who sent you?' the dog asked huskily.
'No one. I came myself,' said Ted gently.

Compare your sentences with those on page 15.

Novel: *Very Best Friend*

Verb Tenses

You can write about events which have happened in the past. You have to change the verb to do this. You can usually do this by adding **d** or **ed**.
e.g. *amaze* – *amaz**ed***, *jump* – *jump**ed***
Sometimes you have to double the last letter and add **ed**.
e.g. *hop* – *ho**pped***
Sometimes the whole word has to be changed.
e.g. *are* – *were*, *go* – *went*, *am* – *was*, *eat* – *ate*

A Re-write these sentences in the past tense.

1 Ted _____ (walk) back towards his house.

2 When he _____ (see) Ted he _____ (say), 'Watch out!'

3 The collar's buckle _____ (look) as if it would be stiff.

4 The cats _____ (arch) their backs and _____ (hiss) with rage.

You can also write about events in the past tense using **had** or **was/were**. e.g. And the mouse **had** understood him too. *(page 5)* He **was** tied up in the garden by the front door. *(page 12)*

B Copy and complete this table of present and past tenses.

Present tense	Past tenses	
live	lived	had lived
stroke		was stroked
	crawled	had crawled
bark	barked	
	sung	

8

Novel: *Very Best Friend*

Expanding Sentences

> Sentences can be expanded to make them more interesting. *e.g. Ted looked around.*
> (how?) *Ted looked around* **quickly**.
> (why?) *Ted looked around quickly* **to see who was following him.**

A Expand these sentences from *Very Best Friend* to answer the questions in brackets. Write your new sentences.

1. So _____ that afternoon, Ted consulted Mouse.
   (**when?**) (page 13)

2. Ted scattered _____ breadcrumbs on the _____ ground.
   (**what sort? what is it like?**) (page 22)

3. The _____ man went back into the house and slammed the door _____ .
   (**what sort? why?**) (page 32)

4. He ran straight to the police station _____ .
   (**why?**) (page 40)

B Read each page which contains the sentences above. Compare the original sentences with your expanded sentences. Which version do you think works best? Why?

C Read this passage from page 3. Expand each sentence to make the passage more interesting.

> 'Leave some for me,' said a tiny voice.
> Ted looked round, but there was no one in sight.
> He thought he must have been dreaming.
> He took another bite of his biscuit ...

Novel: *Very Best Friend*

Mapping out Events

A film trailer is a short extract from a film, shown before the film is released. It is designed to make people want to see the film.

A film company has asked you to design a film trailer for *Very Best Friend*. The director wants five shots to show the events in Chapter 5. (pages 35–46)

A List five important things which happen in this chapter.

B Copy and complete this film trailer story board.

1		
2	_____	_____
3	_____	_____
4	_____	_____
5	_____	_____

Draw or write down what you will show on the screen.

What sounds will your audience hear?

Will this be a close-up, medium or long-distance shot?

Novel: *Very Best Friend*

Quotes and Characters

> **Quotes** from stories often tell you more about characters than you realise. *e.g. his oval paws should have been white, but they were dirty and matted.* (page 15) This tells you that Beardie the dog was not well cared for by his owner.

A Write down what each of these quotes tells you about Beardie from *Very Best Friend*.

1. Sometimes Beardie stood still in the front window, but more often than not he was tied up in the garden by the front door. (page 12)

2. 'I've never been to the park,' the dog told Ted. (page 16)

3. As soon as the dog saw Ted he rushed round and round in his cage, then tried to put out a paw, panting with delight. (page 50)

4. 'I'm not crying for my old master!' said Beardie. (page 51)

B In your own words explain how and why Beardie's behaviour and personality change in the story. Use the page numbers above to help you.

Novel: *Very Best Friend*

Story Openings

> There are different types of story openings. Ideas for starting a story include:
> - a character or characters speaking
> - a description of a character or place
> - a description of an event.

A Write down what types of story openings these are.

1 Steaming hay and pools of wet mud littered the old farmyard.

2 'It's not fair!' the cats hissed.

3 The fat pigeons flapped their wings wildly as the ginger cat pounced.

4 The field mouse had soft, shiny fur and deep, brown eyes that pleaded to be fed.

B Re-read the first paragraph of *Very Best Friend*. Re-write the start of the story in a different way, using one of these types of openings:

- describing a character *e.g. describing how Mouse looks*
- describing the setting or place where the story starts *e.g. describing the view from Ted's doorstep*
- describing what is happening *e.g. describing how Mouse scurries out from under the doorstep, making Ted jump.*

Novel: **Mrs Maginty and the Cornish Cat**

Using a Dictionary and a Thesaurus

A Read this postcard from Rosie to her friend Helen.

> Dear Helen,
> I'm haveing a fantastik holiday. You'll never gess what. My family is relley getting on for a change! Yesteday my Grandad went fishing and dad played tennis with me. I've also made freinds with a magic cat!
> See you soon.
>   Love Rosie

1 Write six words which you think Rosie has spelt incorrectly.

2 Write the correct spelling. You can check with a dictionary.

3 Can you think of any rules to help Rosie with her spelling?

B Rosie's dad has written a letter to their next door neighbour at home. Read this extract from his letter.

1 List his underlined words.

2 Beside each word suggest two, more interesting words he could have used. You can use a thesaurus to help you.

> The weather here is <u>good</u> so far. The cottage where we are staying is <u>nice</u> and the view from it is <u>lovely</u>. I told the office not to bother me while I was here. My boss was <u>surprised</u>! Our housekeeper, Mrs Maginty, is <u>kind</u> and she even has a <u>friendly</u> cat called Merlin.

Novel: *Mrs Maginty and the Cornish Cat*

Root Word Game

Rosie's gran has a game she likes to play on holiday. She gives everyone a root word, *e.g. rag*. Each person has to make as many other words as they can, starting with the root word.

They score 1 point for every extra letter in each new word. *e.g. rag**ed** (3 points) rag**worm** (4 points)*

A 1 List as many words as you can which start with these root words.

    a down   **b** perm   **c** press

2 Using a dictionary, find as many other words as you can from these root words.

3 Work out the score for each of your new words. Find your total for each root word.

A **prefix** is a group of letters put at the front of some words. *e.g. **re**turn, **re**place, **ex**port, **im**port*
A **suffix** is a group of letters put at the end of some words. *e.g. place**ment**, port**er***
You can add both a prefix and a suffix to some words. *e.g. **re**place**ment**, **im**port**er***

B Write the words you can make by adding a suffix and/or a prefix to each of these root words. You can use a dictionary to help you.

    1 mission   **2** mill   **3** vent

Novel: *Mrs Maginty and the Cornish Cat*

Adverbs in Dialogue

Characters:
Mum   Dad   Mrs Maginty
Percy   Grandad Rosie

A Using what you know about the characters from *Mrs Maginty and the Cornish Cat* a the beginning of the story, write the name of the person who said each quote.

1 'I did suggest that, Mother,' said …

2 'I'm going to sort this out,' said …

3 'Then maybe you'd like to come out in my boat,' said …

4 'Merlin, come here,' said …

5 'I couldn't agree more,' said …

6 'Don't worry, Dad,' said …

Remember – *adverbs* describe verbs
e.g. said Rosie **angrily**, said Dad **sharply**, said Mum **firmly**

B Write an adverb to describe how each character says their quote in section A above.

C 1 Compare your answers with the story. The quotes can be found on: Quote 1 (page 8), 2 (page 12), 3 (page 21), 4 (page 16), 5 (page 23), 6 (page 28)

2 What does the author's adverb tell you about what each character is feeling?

Novel: *Mrs Maginty and the Cornish Cat*

 The Language of Rosie's Knight

Rosie's knight uses old-fashioned language which shows he is from King Arthur's time.

A Write these old-fashioned words.

1 kinsfolk (page 69)   3 maiden (page 70)   5 valiant (page 71)
2 nay (page 70)   4 aye (page 70)   6 hence (page 69)

Beside each word write its modern meaning. You can re-read the sentences in the story to help you work out the meaning.

B Look at the sentences at the top of the page spoken by the knight. Re-write them using modern words.

e.g. Fear not — Don't be afraid
Don't worry — Chill out.

Novel: *Mrs Maginty and the Cornish Cat*

First or Third Person?

> When a story is written in the **first** person, the voice in the story speaks directly to us. *e.g. I hate holidays.*
> The key words to look for are: **I/we – me/us – my/our**.
> When a story is written in the **third** person, it seems to be written by the story writer. *e.g. Rosie hated holidays.*
> The key words to look for are: **she/he/they – her/him/them – her/his/their**.

A Write whether each sentence is written in the first or third person.

1. Every year my parents rent a cottage in Cornwall.
2. Rosie's mum was great but she was always rather quiet on these holidays.
3. My heart sank.
4. It was so beautiful I forgot about being hot and tired.

B Re-write each of these sentences in the first person.

1. 'No way,' she thought.
2. Rosie loved their house and didn't want to move and she knew her mum didn't either.
3. Her heart sank.
4. It was without a shadow of doubt the best cream tea Rosie had ever had.

Compare your answers with the story. The quotes can be found on:
Quote **1** (page 7), **2** (page 7), **3** (page 6), **4** (page 14)

Novel: *Mrs Maginty and the Cornish Cat*

Double Negatives

> **Negative** words are: **not, no, never, nothing, nowhere** and words with **n't** in them.
> e.g. I do **not** like going on holiday. I do**n't** like travelling.
> If you put two negative words in the same sentence they cancel each other out.
> e.g. I do **not** like going on **no** holiday.

A Make a list of the negative words in bold in each speech bubble.

1. I don't know **nothing**.
2. It's no good for **nobody**.
3. They will not do **nothing** for **no one**.

Beside each, write a word the character could say in its place so that the sentence makes sense. *e.g. nothing - anything*

B Copy these sentences, either taking out the second negative word or replacing it with another word, so that the sentence makes sense.

1. Dad said he wouldn't play no tennis with me.
2. We were not going nowhere special on holiday.
3. 'Adults can never see no magic,' said the knight.
4. 'Grandad will never try nothing to do with boats,' said Gran.

Novel: *Mrs Maginty and the Cornish Cat*

Grandad: A Character Portrait

A Re-read pages 62–63.

Make a list of all the reasons why Rosie and her dad think Grandad is a modern knight. You could set out your list like this.

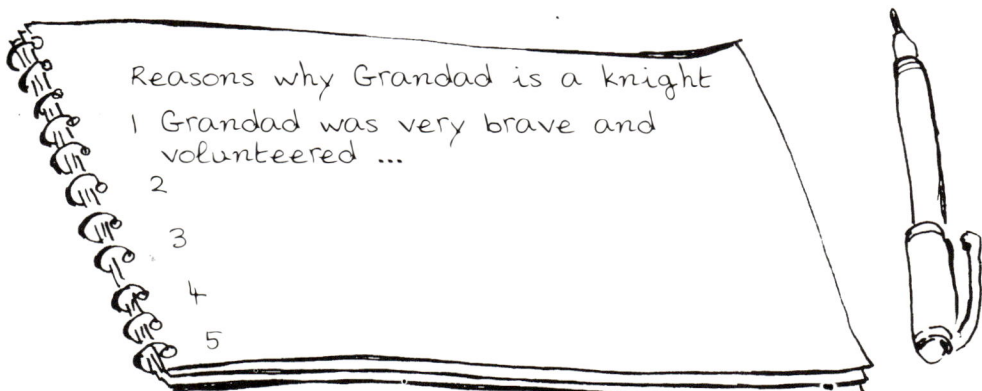

B Imagine that Rosie took a camera with her on holiday.

1. Draw two pictures to show photographs Rosie could have taken of Grandad doing different things on holiday.

2. Beside each 'photograph' explain, in Rosie's words, what Grandad is doing.

Novel: *Mrs Maginty and the Cornish Cat*

Reviewing a Book

You have been asked to award prizes for the story *Mrs Maginty and the Cornish Cat*, in each of these categories.

A Complete these sentences, explaining the reason for your choice.

1

   a   **b**   **c**

The most likeable character is ... because ...

2

   a (pages 10 – 11)   **b** (page 43)   **c** (page 25)

The best description of a setting is ... because ...

3

   a (pages 25 – 26)   **b** (pages 52 – 53)   **c** (pages 68 – 72)

The most memorable event is ... because ...

B Write your opinion of the story for other pupils to read.
Ideas for starter lines:
I liked it when ...
It made me feel sad when ...

Novel: *Mrs Maginty and the Cornish Cat*

Story Structure

Each chapter in *Mrs Maginty and the Cornish Cat* shows how a character changes.

A Make a list of words to describe how these characters feel at the beginning of the story and at the end of their chapter.

1 Grandad

Beginning (page 5)   End of his chapter (pages 26-27)

2 Gran

Beginning (page 8)   End of her chapter (page 36, page 38)

Ideas for words to describe feelings: worried, in pain, calm, stressed, relaxed, happy, at peace, concerned, anxious

B Explain in your own words why each character's feelings change. Use the events in their chapter to help you.
e.g. Grandad's feelings change because …

C Explain in your own words what Rosie's mum and dad are like at the beginning and the end of the story.
You can set out your work like this:
At the beginning of the story Rosie's dad is …
At the end of the story Rosie's dad is …

Short Stories: **Dark Secrets** • *The Mountain Bike*

Idioms

> An **idiom** is an expression that has a different meaning to what you might expect.
> e.g. **getting cold feet** means changing your mind, and deciding not to do something.

A Write each idiom and match it to its meaning.

Idiom	Meaning
under the weather	looking after yourself, not others
grasping the nettle	feeling poorly
taken for a ride	taking action
being under a cloud	not making a decision
feathering your nest	being deceived
beating about the bush	feeling sad

B Write down the idioms from section A which you could use to describe Zak when:

1 he steals some money to buy himself a bike.

2 he feels guilty because he realises that he was wrong to steal the money.

3 he decides to tell the truth about what he has done.

C List any other idioms you know. Use the pictures to help you.

Short Stories: **Dark Secrets** • *The Mountain Bike*

Empathizing with Zak

A Imagine you are Zak. Your parents have found out that you stole the money to buy a new bike. Write what you will say when your parents ask you these questions. You can use the page numbers to help you.

1. Why didn't you ask us to buy you a new bike? (page 5)
   I didn't ask you or Dad to buy me a bike because …

2. How did you steal the money? (pages 8-9)

3. How did you feel when you first brought your new bike home? (pages 13-14)

4. How are you going to try to make up for the bad things you have done? (pages 20-21)

B Imagine you are Zak. Write a short note to Reverend Smallbone apologising for taking the money which was meant for St Barnabas Church. (page 8)

Try to explain what you did and why, and how you feel about it now.

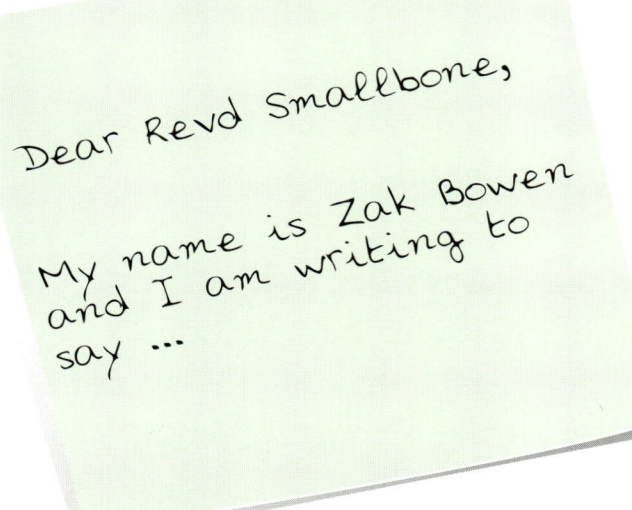

Dear Revd Smallbone,

My name is Zak Bowen and I am writing to say …

Short Stories: **Dark Secrets** • *Thin Ice*

Word Order

> Sometimes you want to use a few words to get across a message, but it must still be easily understood.
> e.g. *Please do not park your car outside this house.*
> *Please do not park here* (use one new word to replace a group of words).
> *No parking please* (change the order of the words).
> *No parking* (take out words which are not essential to the meaning).

A The council had decided to make some new warning signs for the lake in the park, but they need to keep the message short.

DANGER KEEP OFF THE ICE ON THE LAKE AS IT IS THIN AND COULD BREAK

1 Re-write this message in five words.

2 Try to find two different ways of writing this message in three words.

3 Can you write the message in one word?

B How many different, shorter ways can you write this message?

STOP AND LOOK BOTH WAYS BEFORE YOU CROSS THE ROAD TO CHECK THERE ARE NO CARS COMING.

C Design a sign for the park.
Use your best idea from section **A**.
Think about the shape of the sign and its colour, the lettering you use for the message, and any picture/symbol you want to use.

Short Stories: **Dark Secrets** • *Thin Ice*

Simile and Metaphor

> A **simile** compares two or more things using the words **as** or **like**.
> e.g. *the moon was **like** a ghostly face*
> A **metaphor** suggests similarities between things without using 'as' or 'like'.
> e.g. *the moon was a ghostly face*

A Read these sentences. Write whether they contain a simile or a metaphor.

1. The ice was as hard as steel.
2. Terry and Gary were shivering shadows.
3. Terry was shaking like a jelly.
4. The wind was a vicious wolf.
5. The ice splintered and cracked like glass.

B Write a metaphor to describe these.

The wind ...   The street lights ...   The stars ...

Short Stories: **Dark Secrets** • Hide and Seek

Chapter Challenge

A Here are six quotes, one from each chapter of *Hide and Seek*. Can you put them in the right order? You could set out your work like this:

Chapter 1 Quote (4)   Chapter 4
Chapter 2   Chapter 5
Chapter 3   Chapter 6

1 When he got back in the house, Sam told his father what had happened to Sandra Jackson.

2 'That VW's been parked opposite the Jacksons' house for half an hour now.'

3 'Two cars watching the house. That's dodgy.' Mr Bryant went to the phone.

4 'I wonder what the Jackson kids are like?' said Sam thoughtfully.

5 She wondered how long the Jacksons would have to keep their secret.

6 There was a loud, dull explosion and a sheet of flames shot out from inside the Jacksons' front door.

B Write a title for each chapter.
e.g. Chapter 1 - The New Family

Short Stories: **Dark Secrets** • Hide and Seek

Using Commas

> Use **commas** to show where to take a short pause when reading a sentence.
> e.g. *He dialled, waited and then began to explain.* (page 50)
> Use **commas** with direct speech – either after the speech,
> e.g. *'They're weird,' said Sam* (page 45) – or before the speech starts, e.g. *He shouted, 'They are weird.'*

A Write these sentences, putting in commas where they are needed.

1 'Hey' he said as he crossed the road.

2 She began to crawl over the ledge her eyes wide with panic.

3 Tracy shouted up 'I think she's broken her leg.'

4 She stopped abruptly as if she had said too much.

Compare your answers with the story. The quotes can be found on: Quote 1 (page 52), 2 (page 56), 3 (page 58), 4 (page 54)

> **Commas** are also used between items in a list.
> e.g. *The family had seen a VW, Renault, another car and a Fiat outside the Jacksons' house.*

B Write these sentences, using commas between the items listed.

1 The family felt hurt angry confused and surprised by the Jacksons' behaviour.

2 The characters in the story include Mr Jackson Mrs Jackson their children Mrs Bryant her husband Tracy and Sam.

Short Stories: **Dark Secrets** • Hide and Seek

Describing Events in a Story

A Re-read pages 43-47 of *Hide and Seek*. Find phrases to show how the Jacksons behaved, and what the Bryants thought of their behaviour. You could set out your work like this:

What the Jacksons said or did	What the Bryants thought
Mrs Jackson: 'We never eat cake.'	'She is incredibly rude.'

B Re-read pages 58-60. In your own words, explain the reasons for the Jacksons' unfriendly behaviour.

Short Stories: **Dark Secrets** • *Grace*

Apostrophes

An apostrophe shows possession (that something belongs to somebody).
- To show that something belongs to someone, add **'s** at the end of the word.
  e.g. *Grace**'s** fists were tightened.*
  *Jo**'s** lunch money was gone.*
- To show that something belongs to more than one person, add an apostrophe after the **s**.
  e.g. *The girl**s'** bags were in the playground.*
  *Her parent**s'** anger was clear.*

A For each picture, write a sentence using 's.

1  2  3

B Write the group of words which correctly describes each picture.

1  2  3

The girl's bags   The teacher's books   The owner's shop
The girls' bags   The teachers' books   The owners' shop

C Write sentences using 's and s' about objects in your classroom.

Short Stories: **Dark Secrets** • *Grace*

Writing in the Style of the Author

A Re-read this extract from Chapter 1 of *Grace*. (pages 61-62)

List words or phrases the author, Anthony Masters, uses to make his description of Grace sound threatening. Think about how he describes her *appearance*, her *speech* and *what she does*.

> Grace <u>loomed</u> over Jo, tall and gangling. There was something hard about her eyes. They were large, commanding, and there was hatred in them.
>
> … 'Come on. Hand it over then.'
> Jo wasn't going to hand over her lunch money to anyone; even Grace who was much stronger than she was.
> 'No,' Jo said forcefully.
> Grace stepped closer, her fists tightening. 'You want to get hurt? You will if you don't hand over your lunch money.' …
> Grace came even closer and grabbed Jo's arm, twisting it up behind her back. The pain was awful. 'Little Goody Two Shoes. Teacher's pet. Crawler.' The words were harsh and Grace's voice was bitter and angry.

B Write a description of a threatening character in the style of Anthony Masters. Try to include words and phrases that describe how the character speaks, how he or she behaves and what he or she looks like.

Ideas for starter lines:
Tom was mean, very mean.
'Do it or you're for it,' hissed Rachel.

Short Stories: **The Chilli Challenge and Other Stories** • *The Chilli Challenge*

Adding Suffixes

> A **suffix** is a group of letters put at the end of some words.
> To add a **suffix**:
> Take off the **e** if the **suffix** begins with a vowel (a, e, i, o, u)
> e.g. care — car**ing**
> Keep the **e** if the **suffix** begins with a consonant
> e.g. care — care**ful**

A Sort the suffixes below into two lists as quickly as you can:

1. those beginning with vowels
2. those beginning with consonants.

    ing   ment   ion   ation   ty   ance   less   ful

B Read this letter.

1. Make a list of the underlined words.
2. Beside each, write a new word by adding the suffix.

Dear Sonny,

How are you? I hope things didn't go as badly as you thought with your <u>relate</u> - ions.

Here in Bombay everything is the same. Mum and Dad are still <u>argue</u> - ing and I haven't got any one good to play cricket with. As you know Nassar has no <u>imagine</u> - ation when it comes to batting, and as for <u>safe</u> - ty! He broke Mrs Rehman's base - ment window. I said we were <u>true</u> - ly sorry but she was angry that he had been so <u>care</u> - less. We are <u>share</u> - ing the cost of <u>replace</u> - ing it!

Best wishes,

Your friend Ranjit

Look out for these exceptions to the second rule:

argue – arg**u**ment
due – d**u**ly
true – tr**u**ly

Short Stories: **The Chilli Challenge and Other Stories** • The Chilli Challenge

Clauses

> A small group of words containing a verb, which makes a simple sentence, is called a **clause**.
> e.g. *His heart **sank** even further.* (page 8)
> Sentences often have two **clauses** in them, to make them more interesting.
> e.g. *Sonny's mother **climbed** out of the car and the two women promptly **burst** into tears.* (page 9)

A Write whether these sentences have one or two clauses in them. The verbs in the first sentence have been underlined to help you.

1 He <u>gave</u> the bat and ball to one of the other boys, and <u>went</u> back into the house. (page 17)

2 He slumped back against his seat with a sigh. (page 5)

3 Sonny stared gloomily out of the car window. (page 4)

4 His tongue and his lips began to burn and his eyes began to water. (page 19)

B Add another clause to each sentence in section A.
e.g. Sonny stared gloomily out of the car window, counting the people in the village.

Short Stories: **The Chilli Challenge and Other Stories** • *The Chilli Challenge*

Investigating Texts

A For each question, complete the first sentence about Sonny. Complete the second sentence to show whether you are similar to him or different from him.

1. Sonny hates wearing … (page 5)
   I hate wearing … because …

2. Sonny's favourite sport is … (page 6)
   My favourite sport is … because …

3. When Sonny arrives at his aunt and uncle's house they … (page 10)
   When I meet relatives who haven't seen me for a while they usually …

4. Sonny is frightened by … (page 13)
   The animal/insect I am frightened by is … because …

B Sonny has become confused about the order in which the following events happened. Re-read pages 15–18. Write these events in their correct order. You could set out your work like this: 1 **e**   2   3   4   etc

   a One boy taunted me saying, 'City boys are wimps.'
   b Manjit gave me a chilli pepper and told me to eat it.
   c I told the boys their cricket bat wasn't a proper one.
   d Manjit challenged me to a fight.
   e One of the boys said I was wearing a party dress.
   f I felt scared.

Short Stories: **The Chilli Challenge and Other Stories** • *Nomsa and the Baboons*

Connectives Linking Clauses

> When there are two clauses in a sentence, the clauses are usually joined by a connective (linking word).
> e.g. *and, but, although, until, where, as soon as, after, when, before, as, so, while, whose, because, if, who*

A Write the connective in each sentence.

1. All the villagers are feasting now but nobody deserves the feast more than you.
2. The men told how they had unchained the baboons when they reached the mountain.
3. They take the pumpkin seeds and they will not let go of them.
4. Faster and faster they ran until they saw a big, round hut.
5. When he had finished telling his story, the old man led Nomsa to the door.

B Can you replace each connective with a different one, so that the sentence still makes sense?

C Copy these main clauses and add another clause to each to make an interesting sentence.

1. She ran back to the village ...
2. They all laughed ...
3. Suddenly Nomsa sat up ...
4. As soon as it was dark ...

Short Stories: **The Chilli Challenge and Other Stories** • *Nomsa and the Baboons*

African Life

The Post Office wants to design a set of stamps to show life in Nomsa's African village. The stamps will be based on the most important characters, settings and events in the story.

A Write your suggestions for these stamps, giving reasons for your choices.

1. Two important characters.
   e.g. Nomsa's gran, Nomsa, Sangoma

2. Two important settings.
   e.g. Nomsa's village, Mountains, Sangoma's hut

3. Two important events.
   e.g. The baboons stealing mielies (page 26), *Nomsa travelling to see the Sangoma* (page 30)

B Design one of the stamps. You could set out your work like this:

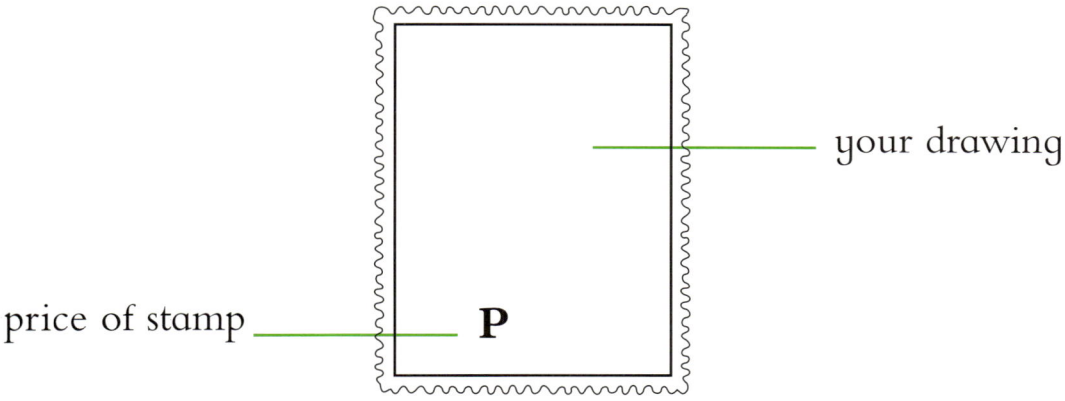

C Write three things you have learnt about life in Nomsa's village. You could write about what people eat, how they travel or the animals around them.

Short Stories: **The Chilli Challenge and Other Stories** • *Nomsa and the Baboons*

Changing the Ingredients

This story tells us about life in a small South African village. The author is planning to write a second version which will tell African children about life in Britain.

A Write each African setting and beside it suggest a similar British setting.

African setting	British setting
1 Village in Southern Africa	• village in Wales • Scottish village • your idea
2 Hut where Nomsa lives	• thatched cottage • high rise flat • your idea
3 Mountains where baboons are released	• Lake District • Dartmoor • your idea

B Write down these African characters and their jobs. Suggest similar people and their jobs for the British version of the story.

1 Nomsa – school child

2 The Sangoma – wise old man

3 Tata (Nomsa's father) – works in the mines

C Think of other ingredients in the story you could change. You can use these ideas to help you.

- maize which villagers grow
- baboons which eat the crops
- drums which beat at the party
- pet goat
- bakkie which the villagers travel in

Short Stories: **The Chilli Challenge and Other Stories** • *A Strange Meeting*

Glossary of Australian Words

A Write the meaning of the following words. Find the words in the story, and explain your answer.

e.g. red gums (page 50) — I think these are trees because Jack says they had 'gnarled trunks' and trees have trunks.

1 pelicans (page 50)   6 galahs (page 56)   7 emus (page 60)

2 spoonbills (page 50)   5 eucalyptus (page 56)   8 aborigines (page 60)

3 darters (page 50)   4 blackened billies (page 52)

B Tick the words on your list which you can find in a dictionary.

1 Compare your explanation with the explanation in the dictionary.

2 If your explanation is different, write out the correct meaning of the word.

Short Stories: **The Chilli Challenge and Other Stories** • *A Strange Meeting*

Checking Agreement

In a sentence, the subject of the sentence must match the verb.
e.g. **Jack was** excited about the day.
His friends were in the back of the bus.
   (subject) (verb)

A Copy these sentences, filling in the space with the correct form of the verb.

1 The bus driver _____ (was/were) pressing his horn.

2 'Teachers _____ (is/are) not allowed to bring their brats here.'

3 'He _____ (was/were) very rude to the men who were above him in rank.'

4 'What _____ (was/were) so terrible about him?'

Compare your answers with the story. The quotes can be found on: Quote 1 (page 67) 2 (page 58) 3 (page 59) 4 (page 59)

When the subject is made up of more than one word, it must still match the verb.
e.g. **Jack and Brucie were** sitting together.

B Decide whether these verbs are correct. For any verbs that are wrong, write out the sentence correctly.

1 'Mrs Rowland and I am staying right here.'

2 One of the bullocks were drowned.

3 Jack nodded, but he wasn't convinced.

Short Stories: **The Chilli Challenge and Other Stories** • *A Strange Meeting*

Different Points of View

A Re-read pages 59-60 of *A Strange Meeting*. Write down what Major Mitchell says or does to Jack after Jack makes each of these statements.

1 'He was very rude to the men who were above him in rank and he was cruel to the men below him.' (page 59 line 19)

2 'He killed emus.' (page 60 line 6)

3 'He killed aborigines,' said Jack. 'That was the worst thing he ever did.' (page 60 line 12)

4 'It was the aborigines' land, you see, sir,' Jack explained. 'The Major was trespassing.' (page 60 line 17)

B For each of the above statements Jack makes, write down how the Major feels:

e.g. angry, can't see what he has done wrong, guilty.

C For each statement, explain why the Major felt as he did.

Plays: **Odysseus and the Cyclops and Other Plays** • *Odysseus and the Cyclops*

Homophones

> **Homophones** are words that sound the same, but which are spelt differently. *e.g. Odysseus was a **great** hero. Polyphemus was going to **grate** their bones to powder.*

A Write the correct homophone in each sentence. You can use a dictionary to help you.

1. At last it was over and the victorious Greeks set **sail/sale** for home.
2. But a violent storm scattered their **grate/great** fleet of sailing ships.
3. 'Bring the cask of strong **wine/whine**.'
4. 'If we **meet/meat** somebody we may need it as a present.'
5. Next morning he **ate/eight** two more friends of Odysseus.
6. As they sailed out to **see/sea**, Odysseus could **see/sea** Polyphemus on the cliff top.

Compare your answers with the story. The sentences can be found on:
Quote 1 (page 6), 2 (page 6), 3 (page 8), 4 (page 8), 5 (page 15), 6 (page 25),

eg. pain

B Write these homophones. Beside each word draw a picture to show what it means.

1. rain, reign   2. sun, son   3. night, knight

pane

Plays: **Odysseus and the Cyclops and Other Plays** • *Odysseus and the Cyclops*

Onomatopoeia

Onomatopoeia or 'sound words' are words that sound like the action they describe.
e.g. sizzle, crack, cuckoo

A Make a list of onomatopoeia which describe the sounds during these events:

1. When Polyphemus eats Odysseus' friends. (page 15)

2. When Odysseus ran the point of his spear into the bloodshot eye of Polyphemus. (page 19)

Ideas for sound words:
crunch, crack, splinter, chomp, gurgle, munch, rumble, pound, pow, smack, swish, splat, splash, crash

B Re-read page 25 of *Odysseus and the Cyclops* in which Polyphemus hurls rocks at Odysseus. Make a list of onomatopoeia to describe the sounds made as the rocks hit the water. You can use a thesaurus to help you.

Plays: **Odysseus and the Cyclops and Other Plays** • *Odysseus and the Cyclops*

Heroes in Greek Mythology

A The Narrator in *Odysseus and the Cyclops* says, 'Odysseus was a great hero – brave, wise and full of good ideas.' (page 6) Answer these questions to show that this is true.

1 What do Odysseus' men say to him that shows they see him as their leader? (page 11)

2 What does Odysseus say that shows he is clever in trying to protect his ships from Polyphemus? (page 14)

3 Why does Odysseus call himself 'Nobody' when Polyphemus asks him his name? (page 18, page 20)

4 What brave deed must Odysseus do to get his men out of the cave safely? (pages 22-23)

B Think about what Odysseus, the hero, and Polyphemus, the villain, say and do, and how they are described. List words to show the differences between them.

Ideas for words: kind, brave, violent, cruel, nasty, thoughtless

Polyphemus is …

Odysseus is …

C Write the names of any modern day heroes who show bravery, wisdom and good ideas to overcome real life problems. Choose one and write a few sentences about why he or she is a hero.

Plays: **Odysseus and the Cyclops and Other Plays** • *The Tailor of Thebes*

Direct to Indirect Speech

> **Direct speech** is when you write the actual words a person says. Put inverted commas ' ' around the words spoken.
> e.g. *'Stitch, stitch, stitch, that's all I ever do,' said Labakan.* (page 28)
> **Indirect speech** is when you write about (or report) what is said.
> e.g. *Labakan said that all he ever did was stitch, stitch, stitch.*

A Write whether each sentence is direct or indirect speech.

1 'I bet I'm really the son of the Pharaoh and got lost as a child,' said Labakan.

2 Labakan said that he thought he was really the son of the Pharaoh and that he had got lost as a child.

3 The shop owner told Labakan that if he sewed as much as he grumbled he'd be the best tailor in Thebes.

4 'If you sewed as much as you grumbled you'd be the best tailor in Thebes,' the shop owner told Labakan.

B Write out the direct speech as indirect speech.

1 'I keep thinking of all the things I could have if I were rich,' said Labakan. (page 29)

Labakan said that he kept …

2 'Choose, my son. Lay your hand on the box that contains your future,' the Pharaoh said to Labakan. (page 43)

The Pharaoh told Labakan …

Plays: **Odysseus and the Cyclops and Other Plays** • The Tailor of Thebes

Performing a Play

A For each of the speeches from *The Tailor of Thebes*, Scene 7, page 46, write how the character should say the words.

1 Labakan: Master, master, please forgive me for running away.

2 Shop owner: You are a thief and rogue, Labakan! You deserve to be punished.

3 Labakan: But here is the robe. I'm wearing it.

4 Shop owner: And look at the state it's in – torn round the hem and covered with sand. Take it off and get out. I'm not going to give you a job any longer.

5 Labakan: But if I haven't any work I shall starve.

Ideas for how to say the words: shouting, yelling, sobbing, whimpering, muttering, grumbling, calmly

B For each character's speech, write the actions they could be doing while saying the lines.

e.g. **Labakan:**   *Master, master, please forgive me for running away. (Whimpering and tugging at shop owner's robe)*

C 1 Re-read all of Scene 7 and for each speech write how the character should say the words and what they should be doing while speaking the lines.

2 Rehearse and perform the scene using all your ideas about how to perform it.

44

Plays: **Odysseus and the Cyclops and Other Plays** • The Tailor of Thebes

Setting the Scene

A For each scene from *The Tailor of Thebes*, write down two pieces of furniture or props you could use to show where the events are taking place. Give reasons for your choices. You can look through the script to help you.

1 Scene 1 A tailor's shop in the bazaar. (pages 28-30)

2 Scene 2 A road in the desert. (pages 31-34)

3 Scene 3 An oasis in the desert. (pages 34-35)

4 Scene 4 Pharaoh's camp. (pages 36-39)

5 Scene 5 Later that night in Pharaoh's tent. (page 40)

6 Scene 6 Three days later in the throne room of the palace. (pages 41-46)

7 Scene 7 The tailor's shop in Thebes some days later. (pages 46-49)

8 Scene 8 Inside Labakan's house. (page 49)

B For each scene, write the type of lighting which would work best. Give reasons for your choices.

Ideas for lighting:
single spot or floodlit, bright or dull, colour of lighting

C Draw the set for one scene, showing where the props will go, and where the characters will be positioned. Write or colour in the lighting you will need.

45

Plays: **Odysseus and the Cyclops and Other Plays** • *London's Burning*

Prepositions

> A **preposition** often shows where something is or where something happens. Sometimes it is one word.
> e.g. *The boats huddle* **under** *the bridges.* (page 58)
> Sometimes it is two or three words.
> e.g. *The neighbours leap* **on to** *the roof* **next** *door.* (page 56)

A 1 List these prepositions and next to each one write a word with the opposite meaning.

Preposition	Opposite	Preposition	Opposite
on	off	up	
over		near	
above		inside	

2 Make up some sentences using prepositions with opposite meanings in the same sentence.

e.g. *James climbed* **up** *the steps and hurtled* **down** *the slide.*

B Find and write the prepositions in this passage. (page 59)

> It rages down to the warehouse –
> Along the riverside –
> And licks its way
> Around the wooden buildings
> Causing such suffocating fumes
> That people choke as they
> Run through the streets.

C Imagine you are a King's messenger, watching the fire. Write a description of the path the fire takes using prepositions in your description. e.g. *The fire started* **in** *Pudding Lane Bakery and spread quickly* **through** *…*

Plays: **Odysseus and the Cyclops and Other Plays** • *London's Burning*

Writing for the Town Crier

In the time of the Great Fire of London, the town crier's job was to tell everyone the local news. He did this by walking around the street ringing a bell and shouting the latest events.

A good example of a town crier's message would be:

Devastation!
Heartbreak!
The whole city destroyed from one small spark.

The message is short and simple. It explains what has happened without using many conjunctions, *e.g. so, then, and*

A Help the town crier by writing a message in eight words or less for each of these events.

1. Ships leave the docks,
   Travel the world,
   Bring back spices, silks
   And all kinds of riches.

2. At two o'clock in the morning
   The dry wood in the baker's kitchen
   No one knows quite how –
   Ignites.

3. Scarlet flames flare round every house and shop.
   The sky glows crimson
   And sparks whirl upwards like a zillion silver stars.

B Write two messages the town crier could use, based on the events on page 64 of *London's Burning*.

Plays: **Odysseus and the Cyclops and Other Plays** • London's Burning

Writing From a Poem

A 1 Write out this poem.

> I am the fire! I am the fire!
> Roaring! Hissing! Sizzling! Leaping!
> I am the fire! I am the fire!
> Quick and curious,
> Fierce and furious.
> I destroy all in my path.

2 Using a different colour for each type of word, underline:
- the verbs (action words)
- onomatopoeia (words that sound like the action they describe)
- the adjectives (words which describe the fire).

3 Draw an arrow between the words which rhyme at the end of each line and put a star★ at the beginning of lines which are repeated.

B Choose one of these natural disasters.
- earthquake • whirlwind/twister • storm at sea • volcano

1 Brainstorm words to describe your natural disaster.

2 Write a poem about the natural disaster you chose. You can use the words from your brainstorm. Try to write as if the voice of the natural disaster is talking to your reader.
e.g. I am the wind! I am the wind! Roaring! Swirling! Crushing! Pushing!